AMERICAN INDIAN STORIES

CARLOS MONTEZUMA

Text by Peter Iverson
Illustrations by Kim Fujiwara

Raintree Publishers
Milwaukee

The boy was named *Wassaja* by his parents. In the language of his people, the Yavapai Indians of central Arizona, his name meant "signaling" or "beckoning."

At the time of his birth, in about 1867, his people were divided into several groups and living in an area of approximately ten million acres. Their lands included several different kinds of terrain. In the north, there were mountains covered with pine trees and beautiful red rock formations. Toward the south, the lands became gradually lower and drier. The southern part was desert, with saguaro cacti and paloverde and mesquite trees.

Wassaja's people moved with the seasons. They knew the resources of the land. In the summer and the autumn, they gathered nuts, fruit, seeds, and berries as they became ready to be harvested. In other places, they harvested piñon nuts, saguaro fruit, sunflower seeds, and manzanita berries.

They also hunted deer, rabbits, and other ground animals plus quail and other birds. The Yavapai made their clothing from animal skins. They used trees and grasses to make their houses and their baskets, which they needed for carrying, storing, and cooking food.

It was not an easy life, but the Yavapai were happy to live in this place. Their stories told them that this area was where they had been created and where they belonged.

For many years, it seemed to be a world that would change slowly. Wassaja's parents hoped that their son would be able to live in a world very much like the world they had enjoyed. Yet that was not to be.

In fact, the Yavapai world was changing very rapidly. Discovery of gold in central Arizona in the early 1860s brought many non-Indian people to the region. White farmers began to move in, taking river water away from the Pima Indians and other successful Indian farmers. And the United States government built several forts, including one in the southern part of Yavapai country. It was called Fort McDowell.

These new people began to prevent the Yavapai and other Indians from going where they wanted to go and from using the land as they wished. The different Indian peoples sometimes did not get along with these newcomers, and they did not always get along with each other. The Yavapai sometimes clashed with the newcomers and with their southern neighbors, the Pima.

When Wassaja was about four years old, the Pima raided the Yavapai community where he lived. They killed several Yavapai and captured others. Wassaja and his two sisters were among those captured.

His sisters were soon sold to a person who took them to Mexico. Wassaja never saw them again. And he never saw his mother who was shot and killed when she went out to look for her children. His father also died not too many years later, before Wassaja could be reunited with him.

Three Pima men took the lonely and frightened little boy to Adamsville, a small town near Florence, Arizona. They found a man there who was from the East and who had traveled to Arizona to look for gold. He also wanted to photograph the area. He was an Italian immigrant named Carlos Gentile.

Mr. Gentile felt sorry for the young Yavapai boy and purchased him for thirty dollars. He had the boy baptized and gave him a new name. From then on, the boy would be called Wassaja only by his own people. He was now Carlos Montezuma. *Montezuma* is the name of an Aztec Indian leader from Mexico. Several ancient Indian sites in central Arizona are named in honor of that great Aztec leader.

Mr. Gentile and Carlos returned to the East. The boy was sometimes overwhelmed by all of the changes in his life. But Gentile seemed kind, and Carlos had little choice but to try to do his best in the new surroundings.

Except for a year spent in Brooklyn, New York, Carlos grew up in Illinois. Gentile tried to take good care of him, but he finally decided to give Carlos up to someone else. When Carlos was eleven years old, William H. Steadman, a Baptist minister in Urbana, Illinois, became his new guardian.

Carlos attended school and adjusted to the white society in which he now lived. He quickly became known as a good student. He worked hard. By this time, English was his main language, and he spoke and wrote it well. He also became very interested in science.

Carlos showed such promise that he went to college when few Americans did so. He enrolled at the local university, the University of Illinois. There he earned a college degree in 1883, with a major in chemistry. Carlos had become one of the few Indian college graduates of his day when he was just a teenager. And he had not forgotten that he was an Indian, for he gave speeches at the university praising the bravery and courage Indians have shown.

Carlos then decided he wanted to be a medical doctor. He attended medical school in Chicago and received his Doctor of Medicine (M.D.) degree in 1889.

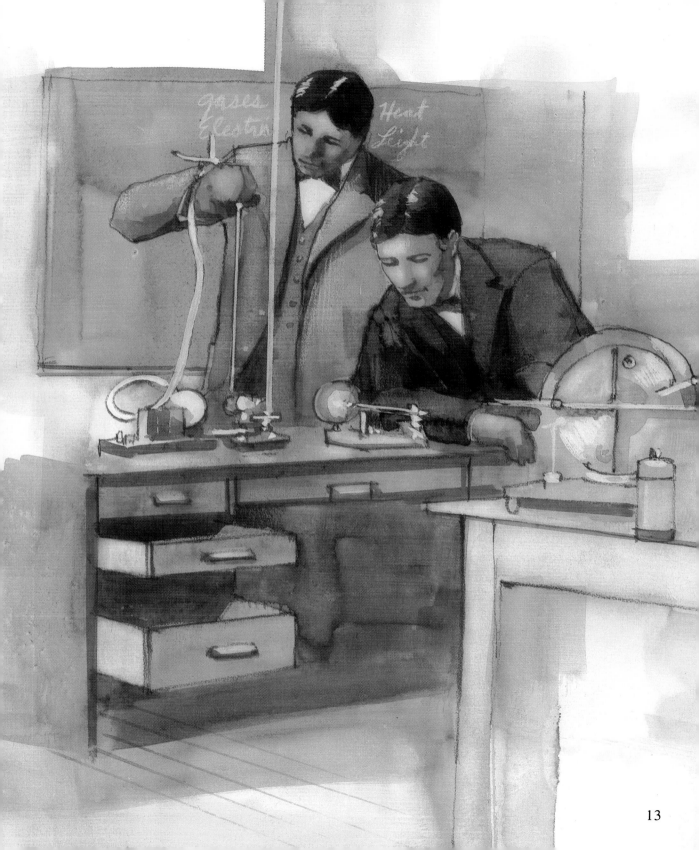

13

While Carlos was in medical school, Richard Henry Pratt, an army officer and educator, wrote to him. Pratt had started the famous Carlisle Indian Industrial School in Pennsylvania. He told Carlos that with his education Carlos could make a difference in the lives of Indian people. "This world is full of work for those who will undertake it," Pratt wrote.

Carlos Montezuma wanted to be a good doctor and an example of what Indians could do if given the chance. After he worked for a short time in Chicago, he decided to live and work among the Indians of the western United States. He wrote to the government's Bureau of Indian Affairs to see if there might be a job available to him in the West.

The Commissioner of Indian Affairs wrote back to Montezuma. He was glad to hear that an Indian medical doctor wanted to work on Indian lands, or reservations as they were called. Dr. Montezuma then spent the next four years on Indian reservations in North Dakota, Nevada, and Washington.

He enjoyed being among Indian people again, but he did not like the way the government controlled the Indian reservations. Dr. Montezuma did not care for the people who were the agents for the government on the reservations. He thought that they did not treat the Indians fairly. He believed the reservations were run too much like prisons.

So it is not surprising that Dr. Montezuma returned to the East to work for Richard H. Pratt at Carlisle. He respected Pratt and Carlisle, for they gave Indian students a chance to learn new skills and be free of the limits placed on them.

During the two and a half years he spent in Pennsylvania, Montezuma enjoyed his friendship with Pratt. He was also glad to meet other people in the East and talk with them about Indian life. He spoke at various conferences about American Indians, and he attended the nation's most important Indian conference held annually in New York State near Lake Mohonk.

In 1897, he decided to return to Chicago. Dr. Montezuma opened an office on the south side of the city, where he also lived. He often gladly saw patients who were not able to pay for his services. He was more interested in being a good doctor than in becoming a wealthy man.

At this time, Dr. Montezuma fell in love with an Indian woman he had met while living in the East. She was a Yankton Sioux named *Zitkala-sa.* Her English name was Gertrude Simmons. She was a fine writer and violinist.

She and Montezuma became engaged, but they did not get married. Gertrude Simmons wanted Montezuma to live with her on the Yankton reservation, so she could be near her aging mother. Montezuma did not want to do so. He had had enough of reservation life. So she broke off the engagement and married a Sioux man. Later she became well known for her writings about Indians.

Although he was living in Chicago, Dr. Montezuma remained very concerned about Indians. His articles about them were published in newspapers. In these articles and in speeches he gave, he talked about the period in which they were living as a time of change. Many of the old Indian ways could no longer work. The reservation system was not a good one. Indians had to find new ways of living in modern America.

At the start of the twentieth century, Dr. Montezuma began to be reintroduced to the land of his birth. In 1900, he traveled to Arizona as the physician for the Carlisle football team when they played the Phoenix Indian School.

He was very pleased by his trip to Arizona, but he wanted to go back for a longer visit. He returned in 1901. This time he stayed with his relatives. He had been writing to some of his cousins, and through them he started to learn more about the Yavapai. His interest in their welfare grew.

At a time when many Indians were losing their lands, some of the Yavapai had gained a new home for themselves. The land around the abandoned Fort McDowell had been set aside for them. President Theodore Roosevelt issued an executive order in September 1903, creating the Fort McDowell Reservation. It was a good place with water from the Verde River flowing through the 25,000-acre reservation.

Because of the water, the land was valuable. The Yavapai knew that they would have to work hard to protect their land and water from non-Indians who would want to take these things from them.

They needed a spokesperson. They needed someone who could talk to government officials. The Yavapai wanted a person who understood them and who would not be afraid to stand up and speak out. They found that person in Carlos Montezuma.

They were lucky to find him. During the rest of his life, Carlos Montezuma stood up and demanded to be heard. He defended the Yavapai, and he spoke out for the Indians' rights to land and water. Even though he did not like the reservations, he believed that the Yavapai deserved a home and that they deserved justice. He helped them defeat efforts to move them off their land.

Montezuma was lucky, too. The Yavapai people gradually changed the way that Montezuma thought about things. If in some way he taught his people, they taught him, too. They taught him about the problems they faced, but they also taught him about the value of living together as a community. He began to understand that the reservation was becoming a home for the people who lived there. Coming to Fort McDowell made him remember the beauty of the people's land and sky.

He brought this new understanding to his work with other Indians. He helped start a new group for American Indians in 1911. It was called the Society of American Indians. The organization held a meeting each year and published a magazine with information about the main issues of the day that got people talking.

Montezuma had strong opinions. For example, he believed that the Bureau of Indian Affairs could not be changed to make it serve the Indians better. It had too many problems. He thought it should be abolished.

Because he felt so strongly, he started his own newspaper so that people all over America could know his opinions. He named the newspaper *Wassaja.* Beginning in April 1916, he published *Wassaja* once a month. It had no advertisements. Montezuma paid for it completely by himself. He called the newspaper "freedom's signal for the Indian."

Not everyone liked what they read in the *Wassaja.* Montezuma was very unpopular with the people he criticized in his paper. These people also did not like the influence he had with the Indians of central and southern Arizona.

Montezuma tried to do his best for Fort McDowell and other Indian communities. Other tribes, even the Pima who had captured him when he was a boy, turned to him now for help.

He spent some of his time in Arizona and some of it in Chicago. Montezuma married Marie Keller in September, 1913. She was from Chicago. They were married by William Steadman, the same Baptist minister who had been Carlos's guardian in Urbana. The Montezuma home in Chicago became a place where Indians traveling to and through the city could stop and feel welcome.

In the final years of his life, Carlos Montezuma worked very hard for the Yavapai and other Indians. He told the people not to be discouraged. In the last issue of *Wassaja*, he said " . . . if the world be against us, let us not be dismayed, let us not be discouraged, let us look up and go ahead and fight on for freedom and citizenship for our people."

In 1922, Dr. Montezuma became seriously ill. He had tuberculosis. As a doctor, he knew he might not survive. He decided to return one last time to his home country. He took the train to Arizona in December.

At Fort McDowell, he stayed with his relatives. There he grew weaker. Marie Montezuma and his relatives were with him when he died on January 31, 1923. At his request, he was buried in the Yavapai cemetery at Fort McDowell.

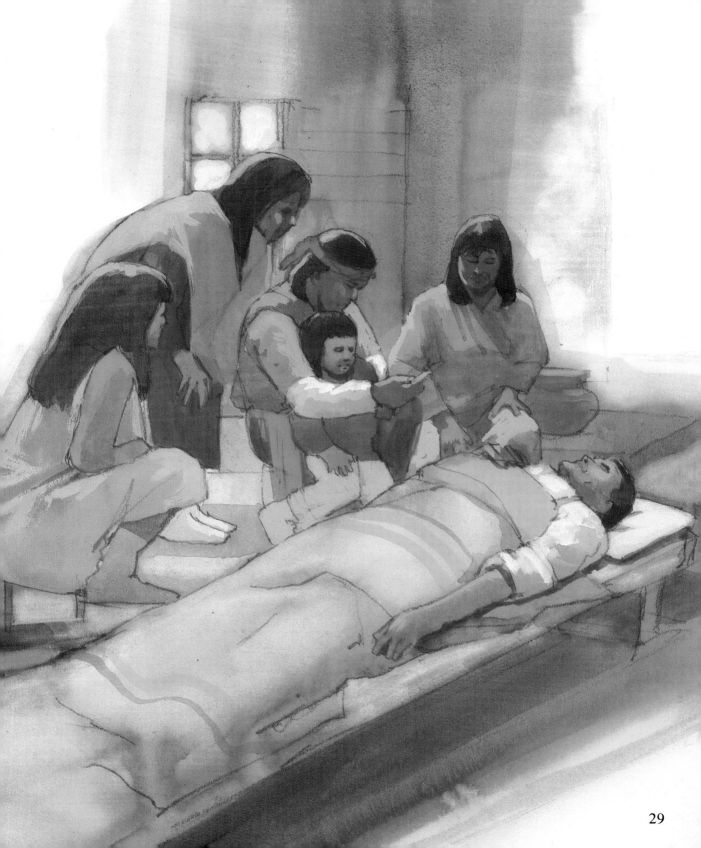

In his life, Carlos Montezuma made a difference. He is remembered for his courage, his determination, and his dedication to his people and to all Indians.

The Yavapai know, too, that by returning home for his final days, Carlos Montezuma paid a special tribute to them and their country. Even now his memory helps inspire them to protect their land and to believe in their future.

A few years ago there were plans to build a dam that would have flooded most of the Fort McDowell land. The Yavapai are not wealthy people, and they were offered a great deal of money to agree to have the dam built.

They voted to turn down the money and protect their land. Some of them said that they fought all the harder to save their land because of the kind of person Carlos Montezuma had been. And they won the battle.

The Yavapai still live at Fort McDowell. They can still look up at the beauty of Four Peaks where Montezuma liked to walk to see his people's land and sky.

HISTORY OF CARLOS MONTEZUMA

1867   Wassaja (Carlos Montezuma) was born. The United States purchased Alaska from Russia.

1871   Wassaja was captured by the Pima Indians and sold to Carlos Gentile who renamed him Carlos Montezuma.

1878   Carlos Montezuma is adopted by William H. Steadman. Thomas Edison patented the phonograph.

1883   Carlos Montezuma earned a college degree from the University of Illinois.

1889   Carlos Montezuma received his Doctor of Medicine (M.D.) degree.

1900-1901   Carlos Montezuma returned to Arizona where he learned more about his family and the Yavapai.

1903   The Fort McDowell Reservation was established for the Yavapai. Orville and Wilbur Wright made their first successful airplane flight.

1911   Carlos Montezuma helped start the Society of American Indians.

1913   Carlos Montezuma married Marie Keller.

1916   Carlos Montezuma began publication of his newspaper *(Wassaja)*.

1923   Carlos Montezuma died. Calvin Coolidge became president when President Warren G. Harding died during his trip home from Alaska.

GENERAL EDITOR
Herman J. Viola
Author of *Exploring the West* and other volumes on the West
and American Indians

MANAGING EDITOR
Robert M. Kvasnicka
Coeditor of *The Commissioners of Indian Affairs, 1824-1977*
Coeditor of *Indian-White Relations: A Persistent Paradox*

MANUSCRIPT EDITOR
Barbara J. Behm

DESIGNER
Kathleen A. Hartnett

PRODUCTION
Andrew Rupniewski
Eileen Rickey

Library of Congress Number: 89-10520

1 2 3 4 5 6 7 8 9   95 94 93 92 91 90 89

Library of Congress Cataloging-in-Publication Data

Iverson, Peter.
    Carlos Montezuma.
    (Raintree American Indian stories)
    Summary: A biography of the Yavapai Indian who became an
important advocate of Indian rights, earned a medical degree, and
founded the Society of American Indians.
    1. Montezuma, Carlos, 1867-1923—Juvenile literature.
2. Yavapai Indians—Biography—Juvenile literature.   3. Indians of
North America—Southwest, New—Biography.   [1. Montezuma,
Carlos, 1867-1923—Juvenile literature.   2. Yavapai Indians—
Biography—Juvenile literature.   3. Indians of North America—
Southwest, New—Biography.   4. Physicians] I. Title. II. Series.
E99.Y5M6533 1989   979′.00497502   [B]   [92]   89-10520
ISBN 0-8172-3408-X (lib. bdg.)

To the Reader . . .

The **Raintree/Rivilo American Indian Stories** series
features the lives of American Indian men and women
important in the history of their tribes. Our purpose is to
provide young readers with accurate accounts of the lives of
these individuals. The stories are written by scholars, including
American Indians.

Indians are as much a part of American life today as they
were one hundred years ago. Even in times past, Indians were
not all the same. Not all of them lived in tepees or wore feather
warbonnets. They were not all warriors. Some did fight against
the white man, but many befriended him.

Whether patriot or politician, athlete or artist, Arapaho or
Zuni, the story of each person in this series deserves to be told.
Whether the individuals gained distinction on the battlefield or
the playing field, in the courtroom or the classroom, they have
enriched the heritage and history of all Americans. It is hoped
that those who read their stories will realize that many different
peoples, regardless of culture or color, have played a part in
shaping the United States, in making America the great country
that it is today.

Herman J. Viola
General Editor
Author of *Exploring the West*
and other volumes on the West
and American Indians